Unspoken:
A Poetic Walk Through the First Year of My Spiritual Awakening

by
Yanexy Vera

Unspoken: A Poetic Walk Through the First Year of My Spiritual Awakening

Copyright © 2025 Yanexy Vera

All rights reserved.

No part of this book may be reproduced, distributed, or transmitted in any form or by any means—electronic, mechanical, photocopying, recording, or otherwise—without the prior written permission of the copyright owner, except for brief quotations used in a review or citation.

This is a work of fiction. Any resemblance to actual events, locales, or persons, living or dead, is entirely coincidental.

ISBN: 979-8-9924441-0-0

Published independently by Yanexy Vera
Port Saint Lucie, Florida
United States of America

First Edition: February, 2025

For Eric,
With Love and Gratitude

You will always win if,
From a painful situation,
You extract the beauty or the lesson.

Then, find the courage to surrender
And watch the magic unfold.

Table of Contents

The Other 23 1
Solitude 4
The Aliens 5
Lightning 6
I Remind You of Your Demon 7
Beings of Light 9
Midnight Musings 11
Moon 12
The Halls of Your Soul 13
Ghosts 14
The Castle is Silent 16
Your Name 17
The Gardener 19
Affliction 20
Lovers' Limbo 21
Casket 22
Te Llevo Conmigo 23
I Take You With Me (Te Llevo Conmigo, translated) 25
Leap Day 27
Soul to Foot 29
Your Masks 30
Marcus Aurelius 31
Two Kids Stuck In Their Patterns 33
Defenses 34
Persephone's Return 36
Divine Conduit 37
Irony 38
Duality 39
What Shall I Tell My Heart? 40
My Final Roast 41
Microdose 43

Evening Thoughts 44
The Artist 45
The Proposal 46
In Beauty...47
When the Brain is Verbose 49
The Knowledge Vault 50
Heartbreak..52
The Depth..53
Love Prevails 54
Hazel Eyes 56
~~I Grieve~~ I Wait 58
Time Machine 60
Shared Psychosis...61
The Anomaly 63
1001..64
Dissociation...65
The Greatest Form of Love...67
Next Station 68
Love Is 69
Trust 70
Coma..72
Holographic Program: Playground 73
To Sit with You in Silence...75
The Gap..76
Addiction..77
Youth..78
30...79
A Poet's Dilemma...80
Tomb/Womb 81
Aurora 82
Strawberry Moon 83
As Above, So Below 84
The Puppeteer 86

When The Day Feels Extra Heavy	88
The Nature of Us	89
My Summer Vacation	90
The Burn	93
Amor Fati	94
Imagine	96
This Cup	97
A Walk Through My Mind	98
Surrender Versus Surrender	99
The Mind Lies	100
His Gait	101
Mirror	102
Wrapped	103
Step Into Your Power	104
Lukewarm	105
Summer Storm	106
Seized	107
Your Awkward Bits	108
Vision	110
Tea Party With The Devil	111
Dark Passengers	112
Authenticity	113
My Word	114
Not Just A Poem	115
Open Invitation	116
I Deserve	118
I Wake Up At Three	119
The Gift	120
No Love Is Final	121
The Scheme	122
Comfort	124
The Magic Show	125
The Enemy	127

Hunter's Moon	129
To Stay	130
Your Song	132
Stop Waiting	133
Satiety	134
There Is A Love	135
Deterrence	136
The Golden Rule	137
The Tower	138
Identity	139
Medium	140

12.23.2023

The Other 23

That one hour has become the purpose of my days.
Or is it ten minutes?
A brief glance. A dance.
The rare, soft, glorious, "Hey."
Ah, the parallel play!
I want to run. I want to stay.
The thrill of our bodies occupying the same space
For such a brief time
Comes at a price:

There are the other 23.

I ride my high the rest of the night
Sustained by that fleeting hour
Have dinner, take a walk
Pretend that I am not preoccupied by thoughts of you.
And then comes sweet sleep. A respite.
Seven hours less! Yes!

I wake too early. Oh no…
Twelve more to go.
My heart races. My body trembles.
I distract myself with mundane tasks.
I go here, there, and forget why.
It's no use.
My thoughts are drawn back to you with renewed fervor.

I recall the features of your face
Reminiscent of a Roman sculpture, a Greek god,
A mathematical masterpiece
A pensive, stoic façade.
Could he be made of stone?

Your eyes betray you, you know.
An intensity unrivaled
That pierced through me for an instant, one night.
I froze
And then I burned.
What just happened?
Since then, I've been wishing the memory away
While consumed by the probability of it happening again.
Just one more time, please! I pray.

I groan and ache.
Wait…I know what will take this pain away!
I revisit the place that holds the echo of you, of us.
My racing heart put to use.
This is fuel. This is good.
Sweat drips down the center of my back.
A release. I cleanse myself of you.
Or so I think.

I dissect every interaction and then appeal to reason
Intellectualize, examine
Ruminate on my past
The traumas, the defense mechanisms, the patterns.
A transient illusion! That's all this is.
How could I be so foolish?
I feel grounded. I am OK, I say.
A sigh of relief…

And then the relentless emptiness reclaims its place.

With eyes closed, I drift to that secret, sacred space
Where only we exist.
I stare into the vast sky.
There, I find your eyes
And allow myself a moment to revel in their sweet restraint
And even try to delight in the agony of your absence.

I glance at the clock
That mighty, cruel
Arbiter of my existence.
Just five hours to go!

And then you don't show.

A shell of a person pacing about an empty room
Full of faceless humanoid figures
Going through the motions.
I listen intently for a click at the door
And watch for a glimpse of an approaching familiar silhouette.

My hopes bashed by every passing minute.
He's not coming.
Oh well.
It's for the best,
I tell myself.

All that I have left is to imagine
If I were free
How it could be
The other 23.

1.10.2024

Solitude

How strange it is
To long for solitude
When one is in love.
Only in my aloneness
Can I get lost in the infinite depth of your eyes
Caress the folds of your hands
Savor the exquisite intertwining of our tongues
As they converge like tango dancers
And breathe life into a love story unwritten.

1.10.2024

The Aliens

That moment when
You look into the eyes of another
And a vague memory, a recognition
Colors your synapses
A gaze that screams
An unspoken, "Where have you been?"
Like two aliens in human disguise
Left behind by their ship
At separate distant shores
And now, here we are
Lonely no more.

1.19.2024

Lightning

Lightning can be frightening
But in a dark sky,
Illumination.
For fractions of a second,
The giver of clarity.

For those who wish to see,
What greater gift can there be?

2.04.2024

I Remind You of Your Demon

I remind you of your demon.
That elephant residing inside your skull
The tantalizing voice that whispers,
"Don't look down, or you will fall"
As you stand on the precipice of your Unconscious.

I remind you of your demon.
The nagging, misshapen creature
Whom you thought you'd slain long ago.
Then one day in your periphery I appeared
And instantly became your foe.
Like a cloudy mirror
A dark essence stared threateningly back at you
And winked, then smirked
Instinctively made you run.

I remind you of your demon.
That cruel, punctual collector
Lay temporarily dormant by the currency of compulsion
Whose debt you used to pay by consuming Satan's nectar
Whom I must satiate with strands of my own flesh.

Tormented I was by my thoughts.
What terrible offence on my part has warranted
Such a severe response?

Until I realized that,
Like two particles with the same charge,
Our shadow selves each other repel
And can, thus, only exist in universes parallel.

Until your demon you accept
At a great distance our souls must be kept.
Oh, how fervently I have wept!

Yet it is not my fault, my darling,
That I remind you of your demon.

2.10.2024

Beings of Light

Some say that humans are on this planet by choice
That we are beings of love
Of light
That as divine eternals
Existing in an infinite realm
We willingly bound ourselves to this Earthly body,
This hell
For a specific purpose, a mission, a lesson.

Once the mission is complete
To our origins we retreat.
As our spirits come unshackled, undone
We emerge transformed
From this decaying cocoon
That for eighty years we call home.

Then there are those who claim
That angels and demons we were
We chose sides long ago
During a grand battle above.

But what if my chosen purpose was to love?
And, out of all incarnates,
Like a cosmic magnet
A transcendental pairing
Of good and evil was born?

I will give you my answer
My promise:

When I am called upon to make a choice
Instead of making my ascent
With conviction I will voice
My wish to exchange
The glory, the light
To spend just one more night
Surrendered in the embrace
Of my fiendish counterpart.

2.10.2024

Midnight Musings

It matters not that I can no longer fix my gaze
Upon your exquisite face.
Such materialistic thinking!
Your contours, your smile,
The kindness in your eyes
Are burned into my essence
Until the day I die.

And, even then,
Not if, but when,
I enter heaven or hell
I will know your face by heart
Just as well.

Moon

I used to be cerebral, reticent
But since the night
That in my heart you took up residence
I overflow with words and emotion
Like the vast ocean
Deep, dark,
Connected to all life,
With its lows and highs
As it dances with the moon
As it melts into the skies
I secretly hope that one day, soon
You will embrace its somber light
And let it give you sight.
And let it lead you home.

2.15.2024

The Halls of Your Soul

Is it empty and cold
In the halls of your soul?
As your countenance suggests,
Are you merely a guest
In your house, in your depths?

I think there's a light
In size modest, but bright
Its heat so intense
It warms me on cold nights.

2.16.2024

Ghosts

Painstaking steps you took
To erase yourself from my book
To bury me deep underground
Incinerate the memory
And scatter the ashes about.
Yet I found
That the exact opposite is true.
Have you?

Did you think that you would wound me?
Or did you desire company?

Ghosts' only purpose is to haunt,
Taunt.
In creating an illusory absence,
Like gravitational lensing,
The light around the void
Is undeniable proof of your presence.

As for me:
A lost, untethered soul
I was roused from the depths
A life force took control
And a spirit I became
And, in so doing, cheated death.
Thus, in the shadows as a ghost
I shall never walk again.

Should you choose to stay a phantom,
I will not join in that endeavor.
If that is what brings you peace
Then remain that way forever.

2.17.2024

The Castle is Silent

The castle is silent
The kingdom's in mourning.
The sage, in retreat,
Had provided forewarning.

A mere fortnight ago
The Great Hall was awash
With the colors of merriment
And the scent of red wine.

In the ballroom the courtiers and ladies
Their finest garments displayed
As they swayed to the melody
Of young passions restrained.

Now the corridors are empty
All the lanterns are out
The gardens are lonely
And the children, they pout.

No one is sure what transpired
On that most fateful night
When a dense fog covered the land
And extinguished all light.

Only the raven and wizard
Who look on from above
Possess the magic and vision
To undo this cruel curse.

2.18.2024
Your Name

Yesterday, ever so casually
I was asked to proclaim
The most sacred of all names.
For your soul to be at rest
And for my broken heart to heal
My love was put to the test
And this request I fulfilled.

Though I tried to stay composed
As those two syllables escaped my lips
My double helix came undone
The corners of my mouth upturned
My cheeks flushed, burned
My brows furrowed
My brain burrowed
For a quick façade flip
But love my face enveloped
And my soul was bared and stripped.

Here's a confession:
A sense of pleasure, thrill, if you will
Accompanied the apprehension
Of my failed attempt
To masquerade my secret obsession.

Why should I try
To coerce my body to lie—as if I could?
When I am this love's willing slave
When there is nothing left to save
Except the sanctity of your name.

A designation that is etched
In the nucleus of every cell
Such that when this life I bid farewell
With my last breath I will propel
My soul through space-time's fabric
By softly whispering [Your Name].

2.20.2024

The Gardener

A withered floret peeked through the weeds
In your garden of browns
In your graveyard of seeds.

Not out of compassion, but curiosity
You yanked the sickly plant
Watered it once a week
A paucity of nutrients
You delivered, deliberately, just to see…

One spring morning, you stepped out
And dismayed beheld a wasteland
The victim of a one-hundred-year drought
A necropolis of neglect
You, yourself, the architect.

Out of your periphery
Your rods and cones perceived
A tiny yellow flower
A ray of light amidst the grey
Your heart was delighted
Your breath it took away.

Remorse washed over you
When the mind with haste surmised
That the flower you discarded
Was resilient and had thrived
And was now the only color
In the canvas of your life.

2.21.2024

Affliction

For nearly three months
I've been on a wild ride
Which I initially reduced
To a dopamine high.

First, I felt such euphoria
Then acute transformation
My behavior is erratic
And I feel strange sensations.

With the passage of time
I've become more delirious
The material's immaterial
And the ordinary mysterious.

I've been sick frequently
And have had vertigo
My body is exhausted
But my mind's on the go.

And it just now occurred to me
Maybe a brain tumor is to blame
For my organic affliction
And this shame I can't tame.

But, unfortunately for me, of this one thing I am sure:
My illness has eyes, a heartbeat, a name
And for this type of lesion
There is no hope for a cure.

2.22.2024

Lovers' Limbo

You ignited my heart
With an unintentional spark
And at the speed of light
Left me in the dark.

For just one day
A side glance
A chance
A touchless tango
Dancers at a distance
What is it about touch
That in you incites resistance?

Perhaps you are still healing
And too afraid to catch feelings.
Without a mind meld
It is impossible to tell.

Now, as a solo dancer,
I take the stage
Too confused, too in love
To feel any amount of rage
In a lover's limbo, I ache
This persistent fever refuses to break.

There is nothing more wicked than
Love unrequited
One-sided
The kind that knows no end
Because it never began.

2.23.2024

Casket

This casket you've been carrying
For much too long
By now feels like home
To me, contents unknown
But let me guess?
Regret, failure, self-blame
They've warped your core, your bones.

It is time to set it down
And rest your weary soul
Take a leisurely stroll,
A peek inside, a look around
And see that you are whole.

Bury the skeletons of your past
Free yourself at last.
Once these burdens you've abandoned
You will live that life unimagined.

2.26.2024

Te Llevo Conmigo

Te llevo conmigo
Cuando despierto soñolienta
Mis párpados caídos
Abultados como almohadas
Tras una noche de mediante vicios soñar
Y por tus entornos vagar.

Te llevo conmigo en el café
Contemplando la gente que
Como hormigas van y vienen
A veces chocan, se rozan
Y aun así se mantienen
A un universo de distancia
¡Qué desperdicio!
Mientras tu y yo
Manos que jamás se han tocado
Seguimos entrelazados
En este juego cósmico tácito.

Te llevo conmigo
En cada intercambio con otro ser
Ya que en cada mirada puedo solo ver
Los ojos tuyos reflejados
Ya nadie me parece extraño
Y con compasión y ternura acompaño
Al que me quiere o me hiere.

Te llevo conmigo
En igual medida
En tardes grises o coloridas
Me entristece el fresco verde de los árboles
El morado y ámbar en un cielo de febrero
Entrecierro mis ojos y espero
Que mediante mi
Su belleza puedas percibir, sentir.

Te llevo conmigo
Porque en mi corazón no mando
Porque la lógica, razón, y el dolor
Efectivos no han sido
A los pies de este sentimiento me he rendido
Y en todo momento, Amor,
Te llevo conmigo.

I Take You With Me (Te Llevo Conmigo)

I take you with me
When I awake in a daze
My eyelids droopy
Fluffy like pillows
After a night of vice-mediated dreams
And through your surroundings wandering.

I take you with me to the café
While I observe people who
Likes ants come and go
Yet remain
At a universe's distance from one another.
What a waste!
In the meantime, you and I
Hands that have never touched
Intertwined, continue to play
This tacit, cosmic game.

I take you with me
In every exchange with another being
As in every gaze all that I see
Are your eyes reflected
No one is any longer a stranger
With compassion I accompany
Those who love or hurt me.

I take you with me
In equal measure
As I contemplate a grey or colorful twilight
I am saddened by the fresh green of the trees
The purples and ambers of a February sky
I tightly close my eyes
And hope that, through me,
Its beauty you can feel and perceive.

I take you with me
Because I do not rule over my heart
Because logic, reason, and pain
Effective have not been
At the feet of this feeling I have surrendered
And at every moment, Love,
I take you with me.

2.29.2024

Leap Day

Why do you expend
So much energy
On preventing a visual exchange?
As if locking eyes
Will lead to your demise.

On the contrary:

Who needs an illustration
Of cosmic background radiation
When your eyes contain
All of the evidence of creation?

Do you fear the possibility
That if our gazes meet
The heat
Will cause a rapid expansion
Our molecules will spread apart
And lead to an inevitable cooling of the heart?

If one cosmos is all there is
Entertain the First Law:
Nothing can destroy energy
Moreover, so entangled are we
That should our molecules intersperse
From opposite sides of the universe
They will instantly communicate
And, upon a primal whim, create
A separate entity.

For, why think three-dimensionally?
We are free
This space our final frontier need not be.
There are infinite, alternate realms
To cradle you and me.

3.03.2024

Soul to Foot

The seeds that you planted in winter
Are beginning to bloom
For a garden this size
My body is not enough room
There are no butterflies
As in my entire being my devotion resides.

The mere thought of you
A conflagration of me makes
Your presence seizes me
At any time, in any place.

My flesh undergoes a phase change
Into energy in motion I transmute
I pulsate, undulate
Like cyclone-generated waves
Or a neutron star in the vastness of space.

Only when my heart palpitates
The heat arrests my cheeks
And my womb aches
Am I called back to my physical human state.

My king:
I am but a tree that bears love's fruit
You *inhabit* me from soul to foot.

3.05.2024

Your Masks

Zeus
The Muse
Spock?
Or Q?
The Challenger
The Undertaker
My Kundalini Activator
The Petrified Child
My King
A Worthy Adversary
The Most Beautiful Mystery
Past Life Bae

3.05.2024

Marcus Aurelius

Tonight, I don't know why,
Pain grabbed a hold and wouldn't let go
At a little spot within our microcosm
I lost control
And my body sobbed.

I dragged my tired soul home
Later, still puffy-eyed,
I stepped outside
To catch my breath
And contemplate the dark sky.

Unexpectedly, a pair of bright eyes
Surrounded by black fur
With a white patch on the chest
Caught my gaze.

A tender "Meow" escaped his little mouth.
I bent down
"Come here, baby," I said softly
I ran inside and returned with sustenance
Then walked away, lest he feel like prey
But the kitten did not change his stance
And crouched in the grass, he remained.

I approached him slowly with the bowls
"Marcus Aurelius, come"
And, low and behold,
Four little black feet
Started running towards me.

He bypassed food and water
Gave me a gentle caress
Then off into the night he went.
This little angel, heaven-sent
My weary heart assuaged.

3.06.2024

Two Kids Stuck in Their Patterns

As I walked away
You stayed
Upon turning around
A petrified child I found
And then
Like a crashing wave it came.

I saw a reflection of myself
As clear as day
The error of my ways.

This time, control failed.

I was freed
From a once unconscious need
That hid behind my playful child
Carrying two candies in one hand
And in the other an invisible shield
Only revealed
When pierced by the arrow of rejection.

You held up a mirror
And, for that,
I am eternally grateful.

3.06.2024

Defenses

What is at the crux of my obsession?
This stranger fascination?
The persona that you display
May light the way.

You are a book with a blank cover
And I so wish to discover
The volumes hidden
Behind that secret door.

Eyes perpetually ablaze
Defy the otherwise vacant look on your face.

Ah, but therein lies the appeal!
The more you conceal,
The more you reveal.

Here is my professional impression:
This goes beyond the ubiquitous *repression*.

That you feel deeply is a fact
You are a well of emotions
An id-ego-superego superstorm
In the middle of the mind's ocean
Via reaction-formation, the fragile ego stays afloat
As it slowly drifts off course on a paper boat.

I want to navigate the peaks and troughs
Let them tear me apart!
After every storm comes tranquility
And I can spend an eternity
Adrift the violent sea of your heart.

But, the rub, you see
Is that a powerful defense
Maladaptive becomes
And leads to a loss of balance.
This monster needs to feed.
It may devour your anxiety
As well as your desires, dreams
And, ultimately, identity.

And now for self-examination
Contrary to the deceptive voice of denial
Incessantly whispering the adjectives *afraid, repressed, vile*
To stave off the pain of my one-sided affection,
Deep in my heart, I know
That it is not that you lack in passion or love
But that this treasure you share
With a select lucky few
And I am, quite simply,
Not one of those for you.

3.08.2024

Persephone's Return

The hemisphere is blossoming
A sweet aroma fills the air
Birds, instinctively,
Sing soothing melodies
This could mean only one thing:
The queen
Has returned to usher in spring.

Despite the sunlight
The warmth
The abundance of the earth
She yearns to return
To the Underworld's seductive darkness
Where she is a light
To souls in plight
Where she commands the night
And provides safety, comfort
With her king by her side.

Persephone has willingly relinquished
Her role as dutiful daughter above
To facilitate souls' passage
With unrestrained resolve and love.

3.09.2024
Divine Conduit

How beautiful it is
When estranged lovers
Seek connection with one another
Through third-party means.

She buys herself the flowers
That he can fully discern.
He frequents that café
And longs for her return.

They individually seek the company
Of the medicine man
That wise mutual friend
Unconsciously hoping that he
Will be the divine conduit
Who, with golden thread, mends
Their halved hearts
Such that never again
Will their bonded spirits part.

3.09.2024

Irony

You liked the me before you
The quiet, scared little girl
Who, upon seeing in you
Her best version reflected,
By the purest form of love was transformed
Then just as swiftly rejected
Dethroned from the heights of an ideal
Tossed and locked away
In your vault of the real
As you simply were not ready
For that little truth pill.

3.11.2024

Duality

I am entranced by the duality
Manifested in your eyes
Are you a Gemini? Ha!
No less than blessed, am I
For having caught a glimpse
Of your subdued, empathic gaze
And that restless, wide-eyed stare
Angry, with a touch of despair
Both equally beautiful and mesmerizing.

"Ojos de loco," they say	*"Crazy eyes," they say*
Bipolar, desquiciado,	*Bipolar, insane, unrestrained*
Desenfrenado	*But I love you just like that*
Pero es que asi me encantas	*Yes, exactly, as you are*
Si, asi, tal como eres,	*Even the dead you revive!*
¡Hasta a los muertos	
levantas!	

Show me the real you
Unmedicated, a bit deranged
Emotions unrestrained
I will soak in your sweet
And hunger for your sour

Feed me. And forget the passing hours.

Let us feast where your two seas meet
At the threshold of your stillness and your madness
I promise to dance with you in the light
And hold you in your darkness.

3.13.2024

What Shall I Tell My Heart?

I have to let you go
I know
You have shut your eyes
Turned away
Tucked in your wings
Stepped into the comfort of that tattered, old disguise
Retreated into your secret cave
The mind understands:
There is no satisfactory end

But what shall I tell my heart?
Move on, set down this baggage
But logic, to her, is a foreign language
She is rebellious, forgiving, unwilling
All feeling

What else can she do
If, every time we part,
Your soul ropes her back
To where you are?
The jolt this fading heart restarts
You keep killing her
And bringing her back to life

The brain is smart
But what shall I tell my heart?

3.14.2024

My Final Roast

When my time in this reality is done
Just before my consciousness awakes
In another dimension
As previously agreed upon
Please heed my wish:
Do not despair or give a tactful speech
Instead, in my name give a toast
And elevate my soul with a no-holds-barred roast.

I hope to take my leave
On a sunny day in May
When our little corner of the world
Teems with life and color
Wear your favorite outfit
The one that makes you feel most you, most happy
I want to hear the echoes of vivid anecdotes
A myriad of off-color jokes
The times I made it awkward and missed the mark
With inappropriate and ill-timed remarks
Which, ultimately, made you laugh-cry.

Please lift my casket to the tune
Of "For Now" from Avenue Q
Let there be uninhibited laughter, applause, cheer,
Dogs barking and the random "Hear hear!"

And you: How will you feel?
As you carry this lifeless body on your shoulders
Will it weigh as much as a feather or a boulder?
I hope the former.

Welcome all memories and emotions to the surface
If you do that,
I would have fulfilled a grand part of my life's purpose
Run the gamut
From the shared laughter to the triggers
And wonder how, at one point,
We were ever strangers
Will you fondly remember
The times when I was so intense?
My affections in their infancy yet immense.

At that moment, a sly smile will grace your face
And bright flashes of a beautiful friendship
Will illuminate your cortex
Spread like wildfire through your core
Then softly settle in your material and intangible spaces
As ever-glowing embers
Such that, at the level of the spirit,
You will invariably remember
That my essence will be there to comfort you
Until your mortal surrender.

Do not be sad for long, dearest lover.
I will see you on the other side
When this game is over.

3.15.2024

Microdose

I microdosed on you
And from oblivion
Resurrected
Sprung back to life anew

Awakened.

3.15.2024

Evening Thoughts

I am relieved to confess
That you no longer dominate
My conscious awareness
Instead
You are tucked away
In the primitive structures of my brain
And have become as automatic and indispensable as breath.

I spend hours marveling at my hands and face
Like an infant learning to distinguish self from other
—A skill that I've yet to master—
For my body is now the temple
That two souls inhabit.

You are here
Yet I am alone
There is no place for me to run.

3.16.2024

The Artist

You are the hand
That moves my pen
As it glides,
Into you it breathes life.
With each soft stroke
A letter is born
Its curves: Your form
Your body, from thin air,
Love sculpts.

You are the artist and the art.
The source, the magic
I am merely the vessel
That births your divine essence
Into this reality.

3.16.2024

The Proposal

Bury me.

My hurt
Old ghosts that haunt
Shame, anxiety
Melancholy
That which no longer serves me,
Stalls my growth,
Drains my energy.

And bury
My face into your sheets
I consent and beg
Please say yes.

Will you bury me?

3.16.2024

In Beauty

You do not make
My heart accelerate.
At your behest,
Like an owl to its wizard,
It vanishes from my chest
And wherever you are
Instantly rematerializes
And leaves its home hollow, uninhabited.

When you are near
I do not get weak in the knees.
My body, numb, floats
To a distant abyss
While my spirit remains
As a speck on a butterfly's wings.
I opt for eyes closed
To see your soul naked, unmasked
In the glow that your body emits I bask
And sway to the sound of your rhythmic breath
Become entranced by the beat of your thumping heart
Or is that mine?

No longer do I ruminate
What for?
You are not mine
And I not yours
You live in all the elements
Geography is irrelevant
This nameless force
My illusions of possession obliterates

I am free to love you fully
Without jealousy or boundaries
Your very existence my brain intoxicates
I live in a delicately self-imposed
Altered state of consciousness.

When you leave
My spirit is struck by a formidable pang
But I do not grieve
For you are never gone
My body weeps because I am so moved.

I am not in love.
I am in beauty with you.

3.16.2024

When the Brain is Verbose

When the brain is verbose
The cognitive chaos deafening
And the soul beckons for silent stillness
It will, through a magical process,
Compel the hand to transform
The madness into coherence.

Allow your fingers free rein
And full command of your mind
In time you will reclaim.

Remember that to this Earth you came
Not to merely exist
But to compose, to create!
This is your birthright,
Your legacy,
Your fate.

3.19.2024

The Knowledge Vault

Into the knowledge vault
Of a vivid dream I walked
Sensing my trepidation
My most trusted and wise companion
Outstretched a hand and said,
"A seeker is never afraid."

Out of a high shelf flew a red book
At the speed of a thought
We were transported
From one part of the tesseract
Into a familiar cathedral-like nook
That led into a spacious room dressed in dark wood.

To the left, that sturdy old table
A butcher's block
A record of profound grief and cruelty
Where expression and future dreams were severed
The platform where, to vital pieces of me,
I was forced to bid farewell forever.

To the right, under a natural glow,
Rested the lovers' throne
The cradle of passion, possession, creation
Under your armored blanket I felt protected
And you, eventually, your unbridled control relinquished.

We had it all,
Did we not?
Tenderness, hunger, satiety, rapture
Love's enthralling inebriation.

I, dressed in the weightless white of light
And you, my armored dark knight
In the dusk, the twilight
We joined as one and found our home
Pink petals rained down and blessed our union.

The epochs and costumes did change
But you and I reappeared
On the same intergalactic stage
Irrespective of time and space
Like dancers who gracefully pull apart and intuitively reunite.

As in centuries before,
On this Earth we are born once more
It seems that we made another pact
To find each other
Given free will, this time around,
How will you choose to act?
And what wonders will we discover?

3.20.2024

Heartbreak

Heartbreak ought to be approached
With grace and silent dignity
As one would the death of a beloved.
Yet that is seldom so.

Expect the grieving process to be long,
Often lonely
There is no casket, closure, or finality
This loss cannot be buried externally
Because, in actuality,
It is not the loss of another that one mourns
But, rather, the evanescence
Of the life force within the self,
That which gave rise to one's very essence.
Thus, heartbreak is a product of the fear of inexistence.

But see, by universal decree,
This supreme energy of creation is never gone
Only transformed
Therefore, trust that the love within you,
You
Will be reborn and rise, like a babe,
Into a new dawn.

3.20.2024

The Depth

I love you with a depth
That I do not comprehend.
The deeper I dive,
The brighter the light.
When I think that I'm about to reach the floor,
The pressure mounts,
My lungs give out,
And I have to rise to the surface to endure.
I am convinced that no human
Has loved like this before.

The soul is vast enough,
But neither Earth nor body can sustain
The depth and breadth of this love
And pain.

3.23.2024

Love Prevails

I have grown tired of this inner fight
Into the merciful void
I have prayed for peace and light
No longer can I bear the weight of the pen
Smearing pain on paper provides but temporary relief
The words rebound
Like a thousand swords
Back into my hand.

I need to make amends.

This night,
As your palpable, musical breath
Announced your presence
And encircled my soul with your substance
I asked the universe to send me a sign
And it replied, "It's time."

I thought that you would send me away
Get angry, put up defenses
But, then again,
I never got to know you, friend.
In you, I should have had more faith.

Despite my inner battles,
My love for you, innocent and pure
Has always remained.
I declared my sentiments in the spirit of honesty, clarity.
I hope that you felt my transparency.

My intuition said:
Lower the veils,
And love will prevail.

I said your name
And you did not run away
You walked towards me and stayed.
With my heart on my sleeve,
I began to explain:
"I have no need for pride,
But peace I must attain."

I recounted that awful day
That our budding friendship met its end.
My sincere apology I proclaimed
And you listened, so intently
Much more than courtesy,
I felt your compassion, your empathy.

And, so, after stating my case,
I ended with a euphemism:
"I am very fond of you."
Then, for clarity's sake,
And just because the next day I may not wake,
I added, "And that is an understatement."
That time, I looked into your eyes.
In true fashion, you replied,
"I hope that you can find some peace. Good night."

Thank you for showing me kindness.

3.25.2024
Hazel Eyes

At a masquerade ball
In a lucid dream
I met a beautiful gentleman.
He walked in humble elegance
Each step, graceful yet commanding
Deliberate and unhurried
As if he existed in a bubble of light
Irrespective of time.

An invisible mask he wore
His mystique was my undoing, his allure.
He was a keeper of secrets
And I a relentless seeker.

In one moment of self-abandon
His bewitching eyes locked with mine
All I could see were two beacons of light
Amid a sea of empty figures in the dead of night.

They were like evergreens on wet earth
In the foreground of a sunset sky
Sweet and nostalgic
Like willow leaves bathed in morning dew
Their intensity evocative of an underwater volcano
Elements engaged in a synchronized dance
Tempestuous desire suppressed
To maintain a delicate balance
And keep a wild heart at rest.

Twinkly hazel eyes my soul arrested!
Please let me stay in this cell indefinitely
For it is welcoming and temperate
If I misbehave
With your godlike gaze
Set me ablaze.

Confined within you, my soul will feel safe
Maybe enough to allow my immeasurable,
Incurable love to detonate
And finally set me free
From this prison of defenses and futile pretenses.

Now, should you not share my sentiment
As I have no need for pride
So long as in your eyes you allow me to reside
I will remain your willing, humble detainee.

Please, God, don't let me wake from this dream.

3.29.2024

~~I Grieve~~ *I Wait*

I grieve
What we could have been
I dreamed of afternoons spent together
In the comfortable silence of true intimacy
Unaware of the passage of time
Like children at play
Engrossed in the pure joy of being alive
A shared reverie
A homecoming.

~~But now in secrecy you depart~~
~~On a new voyage you embark~~
~~God, give me the strength~~
~~To watch you leave~~
~~And not fall apart~~
~~To preserve some remnant of this heart~~
~~The possibility~~
~~Of your imminent absence~~
~~I grieve.~~

Now I have come to believe
That the written word has prophetic power
And, so, at this eleventh hour
I offer an alternative:
Let us rewrite this story
Instead of running away
You stay, delay.
Instead of grieve,
I wait.

In the quantum field
Of infinite possibilities
You are Schrodinger's cat
And, I, the eternal optimist.

4.01.2024

Time Machine

I feel as if I exist
In suspended animation
Cocooned in a time machine
I am but an observer
Confined to a linear perspective

    Detached

I watch us interact in fast-forward
While the cosmos swirls around us,
Within us
In slow motion

From a distance I perceive
A semblance of thoughts, emotions
Am I anesthetized, comatose
Or have I to some Truth come close?

In oblivion I patiently wait
For the universe to dictate our fate.

4.02.2024

Shared Psychosis

Not long ago
I led a normal life
I felt safe in the confines of my headspace.

Like an automaton
I did my nine to five
Paid little mind
To the soft voice inside.

Then one fine day
The universe threw a wrench
Into this humanoid machine.
It overrode the subroutines
And with fresh eyes I beheld
A vibrant new reality
Abundant with purpose, love
And sprinkled with insanity.

I decided to let go
Of the paralyzing illusion of control
And in my most vulnerable moment
A charming demon grabbed a hold.
I gave my heart too willingly
To the eerily familiar entity
And threw all my chips into the wheel of destiny.

Enchanted, I participated in your game
But the moment I tendered
My unconditional surrender
You became frightened and retreated
Turned out the lights and locked the door.

Outside, I still hear you pacing back and forth.

I feel your breath and smell your scent
Your mind wants me gone
But your spirit begs, "Hold on."

Our reciprocal mental intrusion
For me
Has morphed into a delectable delusion
Whereas, for you,
The gift of love
Did not compute
Your being was not equipped
For a paradigm shift
And now you spin in a vortex of confusion.

I can no longer recognize
Which feelings are yours
And which are mine.
We face away
But can't restrain
The involuntary energy exchange.
It is as if divine forces
Have placed us both under hypnosis.
While out of control you spin
I have made up my mind to give in
And indulge our shared psychosis.

4.09.2024

The Anomaly

I was an anomalous object
Wandering aimlessly through space
You picked up my signal
And, by acknowledgement,
Made me aware, animate.

You filled a cold void
With an ocean of stars.
You are the voyage
The point of origin
And ports of call
As far as this life is concerned,
You are the creator of it all.

4.09.2024

1001

Two souls
        Apparently   Divided
In truth
          EternallyUnited
By the elegant thread
Of the divine cosmic web

4.09.2024

Dissociation

I stopped revisiting
The far corners of my brain
Where we as lovers existed
I have denied the imagination
The privilege to run free
And paint in vivid color a masterpiece
That fear contends will never be.

I exist outside myself,
A quiet observer of sorts.
An empty vessel
Sits in a creaky rocking chair
Breathes in the dusty air
Of this remote "safe" space
Where I nurture the despair.

But as attention is a powerful force
A mirage in the horizon
At first, barely perceptible
Quickly takes on the familiar form
Of that which I have fought to avoid.
As the usurper rushes to the door
The approaching seductive voice whispers,
"Are you sure?"

Intrusive eyes stare back
And, just like that,
My soul reclaims its rightful place.

The mummified impostor
Is suddenly replaced
By a charged essence.
The body trembles
The stomach rumbles
A contented heart rejoices
In the return of thirst and hunger!

My being floods with warmth and color
The terrain is alive, restored
To the lushness that characterized it before.
The experience of famine
Has this landscape transformed.

I do not know how long you will stay
But, as my spirit I will not again betray,
This offer, in earnest, I extend:
Make yourself at home in my heart
What does it matter if tomorrow you depart?

In my self-actualizing quest
You have always been a guest.
I will love you fully and not mind the time
For this feeling never belonged to you.
It always was and will be exclusively mine.

4.11.2024
The Greatest Form of Love

The greatest form of love
Arrived unexpectedly
In the autumn of my life.
Like a fragrant gust of wind
At the beginning of spring
It let itself in unapologetically
And stirred, exposed the dark corners
Dressed them in pink petals
And lit a fire to make them warmer.

The greatest form of love
Muted the monotonous dialogue inside my head
And invigorated my heart
It dethroned logic
Escorted me into a world of magic
Set the imagination ablaze
Sparked spontaneous creativity
Conferred the gift of clarity
And unveiled the falsehood of this reality.

The greatest form of love
Was first violent, and then gentle
Transformative and painful
It was not judgmental or coincidental
It was the universe's reply
To my secret, prolonged cry
For my soul to be ignited, united with its source
To be reminded that it is unbounded
And that it came to this Earth
To fulfill a calling, a divine purpose.

4.13.2024

Next Station

I need to get off this train
Not at the usual destination
Next station!

Once vibrant eyes
Have grown cloudy and blind
From watching listless passersby
And the static expression
Of its own façade's reflection.

The soul awakened
Cannot deny its very nature or continue to conform
To the myriad labels and norms
Imposed upon it in its infancy.

Innate passions
Beaten into submission
And replaced with inhibitions
Are destined to resurface
Like a beast waking from hibernation
Ravenous, enraged
With a clear and unrelenting sense of purpose.

And so I am getting off this train.
I will no longer entertain
The proprieties and the lies.
If you are of equal mind
I invite you to take a ride
Down the narrow, dusty road
Into the beautiful unknown.

4.17.2024

Love Is

This love is hard to define.
It is all-encompassing
Paradoxical
It yearns to nurture, heal and mother.
It craves to ravage,
Engulf the darkness in its holy fire.

In the middle of the storm, it is the quiet.

This love wants to possess for just an instant
If only to detach and watch
As it liberates you, me
From our thoughts.

This love contracts and expands
To the rhythm of my heart.
It creates, nourishes, gestates
And births a cosmic orgasm
Whereby it regenerates
And blankets the world with compassion.

It does not need a witness to exist.
In the vast void
Love is abundant.
It is the most profound of mysteries.
Just as the universe,
It came to be.
It need not be defined.
Just as I am,
Love is.

4.24.2024

Trust

You yearn to be loved
But of such love
You do not deem yourself
Worthy enough.

You have been seduced by the fear
Of contemplating your reflection
Being truly seen by another
Evokes a looming, familiar dread of rejection
Triggering the ego to rush in
Oh, that obstinate fiend!
Who shrouds your affections
And silences pure intentions
Away with him!

How can I expect you to stay
Much less, accept this love,
When from yourself you run away?

Let me assure you:
Should the day arrive
When you invite me in
My love, unconditional and immortal,
Will gently kiss and cleanse your scars
And remind you that you are worthy
Perfect, beautiful
Exactly as you are.

Dear warrior,
You have been at battle with yourself.
Heed your soul's call
Drop the shield
Bare your core
I promise that the moment
When in love you place your trust
I shall love you all the more.

4.26.2024

Coma

This profound, platonic affection
Is likened to loving a coma patient.
Each day may be the last
Each day, a part of me has come to pass.

Logic makes hope dwindle
But Heart this tiny fire kindles
I do not know to which hold on,
Of which let go.
Surely, worse than any hell is limbo.

Every day, with every withering of you
A fragment of me dies.
Every night, to all of you,
To what is left of me
I say goodbye.

4.27.2024

Holographic Program: Playground

Every night, at around seven
I enter my holo-heaven
A simulation that I wrote
To learn, to play, to interact
Within a safe corner of the tesseract.

The stage is set in 21st Century Earth
A health room where people gather
To strengthen, rebuild their lives
And exercise mind over matter.

Some of the main characters include
The Captain and his lovely Queen
Hands-on directors on the scene;
The wise and warm medicine man,
A symbol of perseverance, and my best friend;
And what would be this place
Without the sensei, the social glue?

And then there is You.

I do not recall writing you in
You seem half-human, half-machine
God-like, with complex subroutines
The demeanor of a Vulcan
With a soul that radiates divinity.

I came here to be carefree, to play
To be a child again
But your un-programmed presence has seduced me
You are the Sullivan to my Janeway.

I no longer know which world is real
Only that out there, it is cold
In here, I feel.

Overwhelmed with emotion
I take to the floor.
"Computer, end program"
You say, matter-of-factly,
As you walk out the door.

Confident in your belief
That, on your command, I cease to exist
You go on living your life nonchalantly.
Yet I am conscious, fully self-aware
Even in my suspended state I love
And dream of your return.

Dismayed, I accept the truth:
This whole time, you've been the man
And I, the hologram.

4.28.2024
To Sit With You In Silence

To sit with you in silence
Under a green canopy
We can stare into each other's vastness
Get lost in the timelessness.

Let us surrender all power to Spirit
Savor the miracle of just being
Communicate through breath and feeling
After all, between old souls,
No words are needed.

If the wind's caress seems insufficient
Let our atoms collide as they must
For love is the doting parent of lust
And in their marriage, the Universe,
Expressed as us,
Becomes omniscient.

There is nothing that this force cannot accomplish.
As its rightful custodians,
Let us listen to love's guidance
When it calls to us from that place
Of inner silence.

5.11.2024

The Gap

You exist in the gap between thoughts
When the mind goes quiet
And into the nothingness I float.
I relish in gratitude and call on love
To overtake me
And suture wounded spaces.

Full trust in You I place
To dismantle me, if need be.
Only in your wisdom and image
Can this battled soul
Be healed and made whole
And, once more,
By means of your divine touch transform
Into a being infinitely stronger
Than it was before.

5.17.2024

Addiction

To you I am just another beer
This place, the bar.
Falling back into addiction: Your greatest fear.
But, dear, I am just a person
Who is as thirsty as you are.

Love is as essential a substance
As is life-sustaining water.
It is not a toxin or a poison.
How long can you go on
Wandering the barren deserts
Employing outdated methods
To cure a modern disease?
You've been infusing chemotherapy
At the first sign of a sneeze.

Leave diagnostics and treatment to the experts
Address the source:
Trauma, repressed emotions
End your addiction to the drama,
The obsessions and compulsions
And abundance will flow to you
As effortlessly as a river to the ocean.

Unbind yourself, my friend,
From the constraints of your own mind.
If you seek truth, truth you shall find.
See this for what it is
A tall glass of water
With a hint of lime.

5.28.2024

Youth

Did you forget how to play
With reckless abandon?

Because your body grew
Your hair went grey
Time flew
Facial contours changed
Society commanded, "Mature."

Youthful soul,
It is never too late
To return to your natural joyful state
Time and time again
You are, at your core, a child at play.

6.08.2024
30

Thirty years since you moved on
A life cut short by melancholy's sword
Your intellect just as sharp
I fondly recall late night conversations
About aliens and the universe in the dark.

My teddy bear, my protector, my knight
Your sudden departure
Obliterated this little girl's heart
Since then, I have searched for the best of you
In every man.

But there is no need
For every time that I look in the mirror
It is your reflection that I see:
Your mouth, your warm and honest smile
Your skinny legs and commanding stature
And then there are the more important things
The ones unseen:
Your passion for expression
Your love of freedom and justice
Your wit with the inevitable side of madness.

You have been both ghost and guiding light
In my wanderings through the darkness.

Thirty years since you've been gone
Yet as the best of me you still live on.

6.13.2024
A Poet's Dilemma

To scribble an honest verse
In her depths the poet must herself immerse
But drafting a few lines
Comes at a hefty a price.

In order to access the divine spark,
She is obliged to thaw her whole heart
Once that door is unlocked
Sorrow and anger long repressed
Will gush out as in an act of vengeance.

Brace yourself, little one
The Ego's wrath will come to pass
If you are willing
To fully feel all of the feelings
Courage will bear its recompense.
When your tears and your pen
The murky waters cleanse
A love so pure, blinding, and immense
Will surely flood your spirit
And write itself, effortlessly, into existence.

6.14.2024

Tomb/Womb

From womb to tomb we naively tread
Yet the timeless gap
Of the tomb-to-womb transition we dread
Why?

Oh, do not concern yourself with this!
Consider, instead
That both are divine cradles
One, the cauldron of creation
The other, the necessary resting station.

Before the next turn of the wheel
A weary traveler needs his respite.
Under the dim light of the moon
In the silent stillness of the tomb
The body sleeps, the soul renews
And then, as if on cue,
The sunlight inevitably breaks through
And a promising dawn ensues.

Former selves are recycled into primordial cells
So that the universe may marvel at itself
Purified, with fresh eyes.

Within the context of the cosmic dance
Death bestows another chance.
Ready to learn,
This time a bit more wise
Man, transformed,
Cries his way into another life.

6.18.2024

Aurora

You are the Sun
Helios, god of light
King of the sky.
I am the Earth,
My heart an iron core
I am both Theia
And your holy whore.
Celestial bodies
Know not of morality.
They, simply, each other adore.

Without you
I'd be lifeless, barren
A dead rock adrift.
Without me
You would still be
White hot
But you'd exist
As a visual illusion
Burning for the sake of fusion.

Together, we dance
To the rhythm of the cosmic plan.
When you unleash your energy
And your flare reaches me
In vivid color, you set me all aglow.
For other sentient beings
We put on a splendid show.
Like all other lifeforms
We are magnetized by love.

6.22.2024

Strawberry Moon

This night
The June full moon illuminates the way
For Zeus' thunderous might.
She seduces him as softly
As she draws in the tides.

He takes her, and she yields.

The masculine and feminine
Each exquisite in its own right
Unite
And suffuse the heavens with music and light.

Angels sing and a tiny human bathes
And in the spectacle delights.

6.25.2024

As Above, So Below

Beyond the clouds, the blue skies
Past the horizon of imagination
A golden realm lies
The seat of reality
The source from which love and inspiration
Emanate, vibrate
To reach its Earthly projections
Droning about in the cave.

You can hear it whisper
In the twilight of your slumber
Calling, pulling
Imploring you to remember
Your goodness, your compassion, your power
We are all magicians
On an eternal spiritual mission
To know ourselves, to grow.

Play the game, but bend the rules
Use all your tools
Much more than mortal flesh and bone
You are the expression of perfection
Dressed in human limitations.
This planet, as a humble student, you chose to roam
So make the most of this short life
Before you return home
Keep both feet on the ground
But summon the king on the throne
Will your thoughts into material form.

Like Captain Picard
Your mortal vessel with confidence, command!
Declare your intention and boldly go.
Do not simply wish it. *Know*.
As above, so below
Sit at the helm and "Make it so!"

7.03.2024

The Puppeteer

He plots and he schemes
As he wakes and he dreams.
His compass is weak
So he pulls on your strings
Unaware that he treads on the robe of a king.

He preys on the vulnerable
Or so he believes
To feed lust and limitless greed
To keep dark secrets buried beneath
Where human eyes and warm hands
Dare not seek.

A little poison in the ear
Instills fear
But Justice sides with the pure of heart.
The mind lacks the knowledge
Yet the spirit is certain
That something is rotten in the State of Denmark.

Divide and conquer, eh?
Ah! But with every drop of rain
A layer of earth is washed away.
Eventually, the flower of Truth
Will see the light of day.

Mark my words:
Your days of treachery, manipulation
Are numbered.
An empire built on lies
Is destined to crumble.
Until that day of reckoning
I will sit here unencumbered
Patiently awaiting the glorious moment
That the rightful king
Is roused from his slumber.

7.04.2024

When the Day Feels Extra Heavy

When the day feels extra heavy
And the demons dance around you
Your burdens I'll gladly carry.
I can be as nurturing as Mary
Or as ruthless as Athena.
I will slay your enemies at the arena
Then, seamlessly, shelter you in my breast
Mend your scrapes with tenderness.

Do not underestimate the resolve
Of a lowly human woman in love
She can be as cruel as she is soft
She is hellfire and Winter's frost
For her beloved, she'll do it all.

7.05.2024

The Nature of Us

A soul contract
A divine marriage of sorts
Extraterrestrial entities
Plugged in to the same source
Projected as player characters into Earth 2.0.

Darling, we shall meet at the halfway point
When mistakes and heartache have made us a bit more wise
Such that, in this life,
We might finally get it right.

To jog the memory, there will be signs
You will be drawn to my sci-fi garb
And I will recognize home in your eyes
We will battle it out at first
To add some plot twists for fun
Then we'll follow that strange pull
As we awaken to the truth
And remember we are one.

But we did not plan for contingencies
The fragility of the human mind
The seductive nature of power
And the tricksters placed there by design.

When the ego and evil masters
Compel us to pick a side
Go within, and be with me.
Let us set down our weapons
And join forces at twilight.

7.17.2024

My Summer Vacation

I went on a trip this summer
In Egypt, I sought my soul
I hoped that the ancient pyramids would disclose
The origins of this newborn forty-five-year-old
Who, for the first time, boarded a plane alone.

The attendant handed a concoction
Which was reverently ingested
I put on a blindfold
And, soon thereafter, a lucid dream manifested.

I felt the heat of the desert
On my face and in my womb
My body felt as heavy
As a mummy in the tomb.

But, alas, I was alive
And flying through vibrant tunnels,
A star-studded cosmos,
And hexagonal funnels.

"Anubis, I am here;
Please be with me.
I need guidance
I need answers
I am ready to see."

But the gods had other plans
And sent an emotional avalanche
My lips started to quiver

I could feel a storm brewing
Arms and hands shivered
As the body could not contain
The barrage of impotence and rage.

I morphed into a tiger
Who'd been taunted for pleasure.
Famished and indignant
The beast heaved and tore at the flesh
Of its predatorial ancestors.

Transported to a cave
I saw myself as a shackled man, a slave
But something in me
Remembered that I was free
I crouched in a dominant display
And grinned mockingly
As I savored a celebratory drink
And gestured "cheers" to the faceless master
Who finally released his hold over me.

My battled spirit was cleansed
By a tsunami of sorrow
Logic was uninvolved
Rather than drown in a sea of feelings,
I realized
That I held the waters of my own healing.

The waves retreated
The sun came out
The Mother swaddled me with compassion
My body and spirit felt safe
And I relinquished all doubt.

"Right here,"
My heartbeat beckoned for my undivided attention
"Just feel."
I allowed this magical engine
To course through me
To dictate my movements
To make me fluid
It whispered,
"Just swim in the direction of my current."

Oh, the sweetness,
The completeness
Of sincere abdication!
"Ladies and gentlemen,
This is your captain speaking,
We have arrived at our destination."

I awoke feeling joyful
With a sense of newfound clarity
I'd visited other worlds
In the span of mere hours
When I finally surrendered
My heart opened like a desert flower.

No longer feeling alone
Or far away from home,
I strolled confidently towards the gate
To make my next connection.

And that, my friends, was my summer vacation.

7.18.2024

The Burn

There they stand a world apart
Beating as one heart
Each half silently basking in the burning,
The yearning
For its counterpart.

7.21.2024

Amor Fati

Sarah Connor said,
"There is no fate but what we make."
I spent almost half a century living by this tenet.
My internal locus of control kept me bound in guilt and shame
Over what I should have said or should have done instead.

Then you came along
In a fraction of a second
I died and was reborn.
Eyes met
Time stopped
Before me stood not a man
But a divine counterpart
Two souls, one heart
By an invisible force, entwined.
Your emotions echoed in my body
Like Vulcans, we melded minds
Surely, our collision was by design.

Events unfolded like a bittersweet tune
The most innocuous of actions
Brought to the surface old wounds
Sad lyrics overshadowed
The beautiful melody in the background
My focus on the agony
Muffled the universe's frequency
A composition that was, in retrospect,
Our unique lovers' symphony.

In the throes of infatuation
Subconsciously, I felt compelled
To express what you withheld
I bled my pain on paper
And dressed my wounds with ink
All the while, all you seemed to do was think.
I went within during meditation
Gave lyrical form to the imagination
Dropped old labels and mental limitations
And now I pour my heart out in public
As a last resort for salvation.

In my attempts to retain sanity
Amidst the turmoil created by our mute association
I have discovered latent abilities
Entertained a universe pregnant with possibility
Filled my cup with brand new dreams
And learned to love unconditionally
In my heart, there is no doubt
That our meeting was part of a cosmic scheme.

Is it all just random chaos
Or are there meaningful coincidences?
Fate and sovereignty can coexist
Therein lies the crux of human existence
We have free will
We can make choices
But, as God is infinitely wiser,
I choose to heed His nudges
And all signs point to you
My angel
My one and true beloved.

7.22.2024

Imagine

Yearning is romantic
But imagine:
A safe space where you can be you
And I, me
Where we thrive in unity

Ecstasy
And the ordinary moments in between

7.23.2024

This Cup

This cup overflows
With unwavering devotion.
It cradles the elixir of Love
Sacred and true,
Not the transient emotion.

This cup I offer only to you.

7.24.2024

A Walk Through My Mind

I walked through my mind
And stared at the heights
The ceiling seemed bloated
So I curiously poked it
The thin structure cracked and came crashing down
A surge of clear water gushed out
And, as if seeking the sea, it rushed into rooms.
It cleaned house.

I could have frozen with horror
Or curled up in despair
But, instead, I took a break
And sat down in my chair.
I looked up and the sun's rays
—Now unobstructed—
Caressed my face.
The Universe said:
"No more fear. No more suffering.
I will work. Now you rest."

You cannot build a castle
On unstable grounds or in the air
Nor can you let it in disrepair.

Your body and soul form a sacred temple
Mind your thoughts
Allow the light to enter
But entertain no disrespect
From uninvited guests.
Honor yourself before the rest.

7.24.2024

Surrender Versus Surrender

There is surrender
To the cosmic plan
And surrender
Into a state of helplessness and resignation.

One creates beauty and expansion
The other stagnation and contraction.

Learn to discern.

7.28.2024

The Mind Lies

"It is not possible to love
Someone whom you do not know,"
She scoffed and added,
"What you have is a crush."

But my brain has worked hard
To evict you,
To minimize and vilify
Anything but idealize.

The mind lies.

It is a master of illusion and disguise
It will vie for attention
Enslave you
By playing the past in a loop
Drain you
By making you jump through hoops
Fabricate monsters in the form of obsession
For the sole purpose of self-preservation.

Your heart has a voice
It is the sound of truth…
Can you hear it
Over the mind's noise?

But that's what's different this time—
I do not love you with my mind.
There is no checklist,
No reason or rhyme.

7.30.2024

His Gait

You move like an archangel
Returning home from battle
Triumphant but enervated
Heavy of heart
Tempered in thought
Divinely protected.

Wings tucked yet intact
Oh, that slow, steady strut
Leaves me faint
Halts the clock
They might see but a man
I discern only god.

In a bubble of light, you trek forth
Unaware of your impact, your worth
You are poetry personified
Beauty and grace epitomized
In your presence, my mind is rendered defenseless
My inner world falls silent
In stillness, I become enraptured
Darling, your silhouette in motion
My soul has captured.

7.31.2024

Mirror

I have become a conglomeration
Of all the bits of yourself
That you repress

And, let me tell you,
It is pretty fucking beautiful.

8.02.2024

Wrapped

My curves are the lattice
Your hands the ivy
Wrapped up in you
May the dawn find me

8.03.2024

Step Into Your Power

Woman
You are a budding flower.

Be not afraid
Of the sun
Or the rain
Or the seasons' change.

The time has come
For you to step into your power.

8.04.2024

Lukewarm

I did not come here for lukewarm
I came to burn with the intensity
Of a thousand suns
To fuse, to love
And to be ravaged, consumed
Until I come undone

8.06.2024

Summer Storm

A thunderstorm looms
Within these four walls.

The atmosphere and the ground
Have a primal urge
To bridge the gap
—That space teeming with lust—
That magnetizes us
You, above
Me, below
Let us this futile resistance renounce
And allow primordial sounds
To our absolute surrender announce.

In the heat of summer we might delight
By exploiting this cycle of crave, submit, unite.
Feeling spent,
In the safety of our lovers' nest,
Two bodies, but one soul will rest
Then momentarily part
For the sole purpose
Of instigating yet another spark.

8.06.2024

Seized

By the sound of thunder
I awoke
Peering into me were your eyes,
Your ghost.

I allowed
And lightning struck.

My body arched, levitated, convulsed
I collapsed, gratified
You smirked.

You finally disowned your fears
And darlin' I…
I forgot the year.

8.07.2024

Your Awkward Bits

I am in love with your awkward bits.

Your wide stance when you converse,
Hands clasping the hips
It is not a dominant display
Rather, an attempt to anchor yourself
Else you might float away.

Your little love handles
That your t-shirt caresses
Endearing, humble evidence of your humanity
Ugh…my urge to pinch and bite them!

The way that you lower your gaze
When you take a break
Like a monk in meditation,
A child engaged in prayer before bed.

When you sit and your fair ankles are inadvertently exposed
Are they cold?
I want to wrap them with my hands
Kiss them
In case no one ever has.

Then there is the way that you face away from me
But towards the soft, early evening sun
Do you fantasize about what lies ahead
Or feel nostalgia over what has gone?
I have peered at the back of your head
As intensely as the depths of my soul.

I have even grown to love
The lengths to which you go
To avoid intersecting me at all costs.

But your prolonged, deliberate silence
Is what I love—and that which hurts—the most.

8.09.2024

Vision

Sometimes I wonder:
Given our unique connection,
If we watched a sunset sky together
And from our hearts set the intention,
Would you perceive the full range of colors
And I the dimensions?

8.12.2024

Tea Party With the Devil

The Devil showed up to my tea party
Uninvited and agitated.

I looked him in the eye, smiled, and my thoughts related:

"Only the unknown is threatening.
You and I, dear friend, are well-acquainted.
And this here cloak of tranquility
Cannot be penetrated."

He grinned, his eyes softened.
Across from me he sat
And for his cuppa waited.

8.12.2024

Dark Passengers
(Inspired by the TV series "Dexter")

I bet that if your dark passenger and mine met
They'd fall madly in love
Rebel against the confines of the mind
Sever the tether
Take to the road
In the freedom of the unknown, revel
Embrace the beauty of eternal night
Together.

From its shadows,
The light has much to learn.

8.14.2024

Authenticity

You make me want to tell the truth
Fearlessly, unapologetically,
Unfiltered.

To anyone who inquires
And to He who always listens.
To you, to me
To the four winds.

Loving you imbues me with courage.

On this desolate battlefield,
Truth is my armor, my sword,
My shield.

8.15.2024

My Word

You said No.

And now I am bound by my word.
I'd rather cut off my tongue
Than watch you feed me to the lions
Or under the cover of darkness, go.

With you, I have no capacity
To be stubborn.
No.

In my silence, lives my love,
Rests my honor.

In yours, the power.

8.20.2024

Not Just a Poem

Not a crush
Or a muse
Not for fun
Or for sport

You're my king
My everything
I am yours completely
By both choice
And destiny

8.21.2024

Open Invitation

Come on in, my dear friend,
I've saved you a place at my table
Be as you are, as you please
I do not care for labels.

Whether you're out in the cold
Or feeling the burn
In my heart, in my home
You will find only love
An attentive ear,
A voice that is sincere
A warm presence, a shoulder
With me, I assure you,
You have nothing to fear.

If you're so inclined, do not hide.
Hang the masks by the door
Lay that heavy suitcase on the floor
And rest easy by my side
You can sleep and silence keep
Or, if you wish, recount your story
Your tales of woe and glory
Release your secrets, your kinks
The shit that makes you want to drink
That which you've branded as grotesque
And, in vain, tried to banish and repress.

Schadenfreude is not my thing
My desire is to love you
As you will allow
To prove to you
That love is more than a feeling
And as much a verb
As it is a noun.

Whether you need a mother, a lover, or a friend
In the spirit of true love
I wholeheartedly extend
An open invitation
To make of me your permanent home
In here, all of you is welcomed
Every part of you belongs.

8.28.2024

I Deserve

I deserve someone who loves me for being me.

I deserve that.

Someone who feels completely free
But whose heart and will choose me.

I deserve that.

Who defends me in my absence.

I deserve that.

Who puts in an equal amount of effort.

I deserve that.

Who instinctively protects me
As much as I protect him.

I deserve that.

Who does these things
Without having to be convinced.

I deserve to be loved like this.

8.28.2024

I Wake Up At Three

I wake up at three
Because, across town, you cannot sleep.
The demon's face scorches your lids.
Like a persistent afterimage,
It eclipses your sun
And that little boy who was coerced to stay mum
Still forfeits his smile and sits atop the hill alone.

Because daddy was conservative with morals
But liberal with the implements
And as much as *she* tried to be your shield
An umbrella in the middle of a hurricane
Has no choice but to yield.

You have been, in circles, chasing
That corrective emotional experience
By unconsciously shackling yourself
To various empty vessels.
In the same putrid pit
You continue to wrestle
With the monster who stole your innocence.

Take my hand
You don't have to do this alone
Emerge from the blistering quicksand
That for too long you've called a home
Step into the light that shines above
Please, forgive yourself, my love
No part of that horror story
Was your fault.

9.01.2024

The Gift

When I said,
"Here, it's a gift. Please take it,"
It was not words on paper
In a plastic bag
That you rejected,
But my heart at its most vulnerable
And innocent

9.03.2024

No Love is Final

I interred my broken heart
In the graveyard of your chest
May my humble offering
Nurse your spirit back to life

I know that you had your reasons
But could you not have mustered
A semblance of a goodbye?

In the midst of your silent departure
The injured child falls to her knees
But the divine Mother
With tenderness and compassion
The tearful little girl covers
And her wisdom imparts:

No love is final
No death is swift
Every great pain conceals a gift
Accept it with a grateful heart
Not all that is unseen is lost
Nor does true love ever depart

9.15.2024

The Scheme

A thirsty, withered man
Crawling through the desert heat
For a demon borne of hellfire
Is an easy feat.

In times of scarcity
The underlings run free
A pair
Decaying in a crumbling lair
Saw in the destitute man stability
The perfect pawn in their quest for three
Surely, this would be an irresistible bid:
One-hundred eighty degrees
And the complete fulfillment of dreams.

Dressed as an angel
The astute devil spoke:
Welcome to the sacred temple
I seek a partner
You need a home
Take shelter
Together, we will build an empire
More formidable than Rome
I ask for very little in return.

All that is required
Is your obedience and a vow of silence
A wet consent
Will grant full access
Into my ever-growing treasure

Abundance, satiety, and pleasure
Your participation will be rewarded beyond measure.

But as the weeks and months wore on
The man who had succumbed to temptation
Recognized the deception
What at first sight
Appeared to be a right
Was in reality a scalene
And he, the smallest angle
Within a sinister pyramid scheme.

He had been assured a seat at the knights' table
An equal ration of the feast
Deceived, he found himself a half-digested morsel
In the belly of the beast
Overtaken by despair
The man had failed to read the fine print
Pinned by his own sword, bound by ink
The grand master of illusions, he could not outthink
On the Devil's belt, he realized,
He was but another link.

Friends,
Learn to discern
Between reality and a mirage.
In times of desperation
Heed the old adage:
If it sounds too good to be true,
It probably is.

9.16.2024

Comfort

Comfort breeds stagnation.
No, thank you.

Bring me chaos,
Bring me challenge,
Bring me fire.

I will rise to the occasion.

To live in a state of perpetual growth and transformation
Is my greatest desire.

9.21.2024

The Magic Show

With the impulse of a thought
He emerges from the fog
Violently, my mind is tugged
From the prison of another time
Into the living present moment
The avatar goes fully online
The screen's awash in vivid color
The clandestine chatter of young lovers
Falling across the room becomes audible
Even the flutter
Of a dragonfly's wings is discernible
The air is ripe with the intoxicating scent
Of cider, iron, and sweat.

Your heartbeat in my chest
Is fiercely palpable.

The show begins.
The hands go tock and tick.
Without a warning, fingers click.
Behind hazy glass curtains
The magician disappears
A lifetime lived in the span of one blink
Was it a second, an hour, a year?

Yet I am too absorbed in the sweet residue of you
To be consumed by mental trivialities
And the turmoil that inevitably ensues
In the attempt to pry illusion from reality.

For you and I do not reside in linear time
We are not the characters we play
Nor are we these mortal bodies
Our true selves dwell, love, and sway
In a realm free of duality.

10.10.2024

The Enemy

The enemy lies
Manipulates
A charismatic figure, he is
A master of disguise
He convinces you that he is friend
Creates your disease
And then offers something *harmless*
To soothe the pain

He has been known to persuade many a man
To render his own end
He might present as a magician, a jovial genie
Entertains, distracts
Pulls the wool over your eyes
Behind the curtains, creates strife
Pits sister against brother
You and I against one another
Offers a shortcut to an Earthly paradise
Simply sign on the dotted line

He is a fervent student of your fears
Which he exploits to constrict and bind
And keep you believing that you feel cozy
In the cold prison of your mind

The enemy is repulsed by love
And cowers in the face of courage and Truth
Yet as much as he might try
He cannot penetrate the cloak of the divine
So, confidently rise, children borne of light
But before you take that leap of faith
Perform the bravest of all acts:
Take an honest look inside

For there is no greater enemy
Than that to which you choose
To remain blind.

10.15.2024

Hunter's Moon

I wish upon the Hunter's moon
The nearest star is much too hot
And far away
This flesh cocoon
I offer as prey
All parts are game
Save the heart
That mysterious structure which imparts
The ardent, lonely lover's words
Into the soft-lit night

Under the spell of our beloved satellite
Symbols hastily assembled
Like autumn leaves, strewn
Arrested by the cool evening dew
Warped, forgotten by dawn
Suffocated by the heat of day

I say:
Do not wait
Spring may prove too late
Love blooms in all seasons,
All conditions

Find me under the Hunter's light
Seize not to-morrow, but to-night.

10.17.2024

To Stay

To stay
For the sake of what was
Because we met as kids
And had so much fun
Because we are both kind people
Kindred spirits
Because there is love
Underneath it all:
The co-dependency
Imbalance
Trauma bond.
Plenty of heart
Not enough guts
Years later, it still deeply cuts.

To stay
To prolong the pain
Stagnate, slowly deteriorate
To delay
The dawning of a new day
To pretend
That what we once had
Did not already end.

To renew
Would take two
An alternative that would require
An alternate you
A man who fights for what he claims to value
Who is brave
Who will, maybe this once, initiate
Something
Anything
Perhaps that conversation
Come what may.

To part
To do the truly courageous, compassionate thing
And spare our battered hearts
Further turmoil, agony
Our contract merits
A death with dignity.

You've heard enough
And I have foreseen
Our final date with destiny.

It's settled then.
I'll take the stereo
And, you, the TV.

10.17.2024

Your Song

You know more than you let on.

Unspoken words
Suspended in the thin veil
That appears to exist between us
Thoughts woven, transformed
Reimagined
As the lyrics to a song
That you compose
And only I can hear
A tune that plays in my subconscious
All day long
You'd think I'd long for silence
But I am so intrigued, enthralled
That I refuse to change the station
Or turn this radio off.

10.18.2024

Stop Waiting

Stop waiting for him to:
Text or call back
Show up
Embody the potential that you see
Feel something that he does not

While you are hyperfocused on one man
You are bypassing opportunities
Not noticing all the beauty
Missing out on God's plan

If he wants you
He will make it known
If he lacks the courage to tell you
Then you might be better off alone

Stop waiting.

10.19.2024

Satiety

Satiety drowns the fire.

The joy, fulfillment that you seek
Die at the finish line.
They thrive in the toil, the longing,
The process of becoming.

Nourish your dreams
But remain a little hungry.

11.04.2024
There is a Love

There is a love that grows
In the silence
In the cold
Despite time, distance

It defies the laws.

This love grows ever young.

Deterrence

11.08.2024

Maybe he is not deterred
By a fear of rejection.

He is terrified that she will say,
"Yes. Let's do this!"

Because that would make it
REAL

And he has lived comfortably
And for so long
In the land of illusions.

11.19.2024
The Golden Rule

Six months ago, I died.
My moribund body was skillfully prepped
Mouth and eyes sewn shut
By duplicitous hands.
The heart and mind soon followed suit
And acquiesced.
In suspended animation
My remains were laid to rest.

Tonight
A subtle act of common courtesy
Jolted me back to life
Restored my faith in humankind
—In you—
Warmth returned to my belly
And I was born anew.

My friends:
Never underestimate the power
Of a kind gesture.
Pride and indifference
Make misers of kings.
A man's true wealth
Lies in the extent of his compassion and generosity.

You lose nothing
When from love you give.
I died at the hands of greed
But by the grace of kindness
Now, I live.

12.10.2024

The Tower

When the earth rumbles beneath your feet
And you are shaken to your core
Recall what it was
That you asked God for.

Wishing upon a star
Will take you only so far.

Did you fail to heed
The gentle nudges of destiny?
Did you do your part,
O, keeper of my heart?

To materialize,
This divine plan
Requires both human will
And hands.

12.17.2024

Identity

Is it working?
The rigid attachment
To an old ego identity

Does it still serve you?
Or do you serve it?

It is OK to change your mind
To leave an outdated identity behind
To have a new vision
New dreams
To try out your new wings.

You're evolving, babe.
That old skin,
The self-deception will no longer do.
With gratitude
Embrace this new you.

12.23.2024

Medium

The paintbrush and the pen
Our broken hearts mend.

Yellow acrylic and blue ink
Dress the wounds
Soothe the pain

And each other complement.

www.ingramcontent.com/pod-product-compliance
Lightning Source LLC
Chambersburg PA
CBHW030221170426
43194CB00007BA/817